Sutras of The

Heart

Spiritual Poetry to Nourish

the Soul

By

Ulonda Faye

PREFACE

These heart-based writings, from my poetic heart, were written over the course of a three-year period as a reflection of my own inner and outer journey.

It has been my personal experience to witness my Soul's evolution as a physical and spiritual vessel of the infinite presence that is in and all around us. I sincerely hope you, the reader, will find solace and healing as well as inspiration through these poetic sutras.

In order to express how I feel our Soul is connected to our infinite resource; I have chosen to capitalize the word, Soul, as well as specific other words. While this is not in accordance with our current grammar structure, it is my intention to let you know how strongly I feel about them.

Where you find new capitalizations and other 'out-of-the-ordinary' forms of grammar, it is with the sole interest to add extra emphasis. My endeavor here is to bring forth writing from my heart and Soul, and for this purpose standard grammar is not my explicit focus.

I am delighted and grateful to share these writings with you and look forward to publishing more.

With love & gratitude,
Ulonda Faye

Dedication

To the One
Who found, saw me
Loved me

Above all
To the One
I melt
Into

TABLE OF CONTENTS

NEW LIFE

Meeting you,

in my dreams

Kissing you,

in the cool breeze

Awaken me, to your colors,

as to feel my heartbeat.

You never cease to amaze me, and see me

as I am.

I love you

and

I kiss you

For a new day is birthed

through the grace

of your hand -

Here, is where I am.

Hearts Beating into One

I am grateful for the infinite, creative living force

within all.

We are beauty

continuously, being carved.

At times, painful, yet each cut reveals

deeper awareness

of our inner magnificence.

We get to the heart of matter

realizing, we are more than this physicality.

Infinite particles found in stars.

Fragments, beaming of light, pouring forth through the

sun.

Grains of sand blown by the wind,

along with blades of grass and prickly ash

from our Earth.

We fly as an eagle- soaring, and with the night, we come to

be

awakened by the morning light.

Glorious life, here we meet and

here, we are One as our hearts beat.

Opening to Love

Everything in life is leading to deeper and greater love.

Love for the beauty and love that is within and all around
us
as too, the love for the mysteries unfolding all around us.
Love within the wound; love within the pain; love within
the flame; love within the sacred temple
of the Soul, and love unfolding everywhere we go.

When we go deeper into every experience and emotion -
especially, the painful ones,
we tap into the source of our greatest hidden gifts.

Come with me, beloved, and dive deeper into the murky
waters,
where only fear shall forbid you to go.

There in the depths, we meet

as lovers who have not allowed defeat.

Our Heart, an Ocean

Drops of kindness, dripping down to another,

as a drop into the ocean

watering, our own heart.

Every river flows gracefully, at times with such intensity -

yet, ever so gently into the ocean of all hearts.

Be a drop of kindness and a river flowing gladly to

another.

In the Oneness that is we, each drop waters each cell,

which reunites us in the wholeness as

water from a well.

Love is the guide, teacher and humble servant

It waters our cells.

Open to love

Be love.

An Instant of Eternity

A song to the skies, and the clouds weep

as if they had been asleep.

Our songs are felt above and below,

and seep into the depths of our Souls.

When I think of a God, I think of giving and receiving.

A deep destiny and song within us all waiting to be sung

as our Oneness when we embody God, and in our service,

we offer as

our gift to All.

Grateful for another day of loving,

and grateful for all for which I am.

Everything is Possible

Dream your dreams

create your art

sing your songs

and play your best game ever.

We are all stars

starring in our very own life.

Everything we dream, think, speak, and surround

ourselves with, assists us

in our realization of our most beautiful possibilities.

We are all equals, uniquely standing apart, to stand strong

as One.

We are all blessed, and we are all here

for a purpose for which only our Soul truly knows.

Tune in

to your call,

listen

dream.

Do only that which brings happiness and well-being.

If it feels good and makes you happy, then do more of it.

Spend time with people who believe in you and support

you.

Be with those who feed your Soul

for, when you grow and blossom, there are fields of

flowers to nurture all.

Wish the best for yourself and the perceived other.

Winning the Inner War

Rise above all pain -

There is no need, to sleep.

Open your eyes, and awaken, my love.

Life is wishing to be expressed through you

as its very own creation.

Wait not for perfection.

Death, the perfected state, brings us back from all wars

with this life.

Here we are to live

dance

sing

be

breathe

exist.

What if, one would fall, into an empty abyss?

Nothing truly outrageous would happen -

or could it finally happen?

Dare to soar

Fly angel fly - Free

For here, we are to love and be.

TRUTH WITHIN US

Our very nature is truth.

It is because of truth that we exist, and it is to truth that we

return,

flowing.

It is true, everything about you

as you are this echo of infinity.

Desert flowers grow and even thrive

in times of little sustenance.

They trust, rainy days await, as they push down their roots

deep

until the skies begin to weep.

Their blessings are that which fall from the sky

as too from our Soul's eye.

The heartbeat of nature is in you, and you are a pattern of

truth

as love beats through you.

GO WITHIN

There, and only there, will you find the answers you seek.

The experience of another can be touched, yet only the

truth from within you,

can be felt.

Do you feel it?

Let it speak to your heart, and flow within your Soul's

river.

The water within shall bathe you

to truly set you free.

Jumping into the waters, let not the depths frighten you,

nor the answers scare you.

For you are the child here to be born -

Awaken my dear.

Awaken to Beauty

Commune with the dew of your Soul,

awaken to all of you -

your beauty.

It is your unique essence that sustains

your fragrance that maintains

in this ever present now.

You are beautiful.

Love yourself.

Get to know you,

everyday more.

Teach your children the same.

The Earth delights in her beautiful flowers.

You are a beautiful flower.

Will you bloom?

BALANCE, THE BLESSING

There is greater justice at play, always.

No matter the struggles we face, all injustices are balanced
out in time.

Strive to do right by you
do no harm, while keeping your beautiful Being safe and
always nourished with love.

All challenges, when consciously faced, make us stronger,
and
with this strength we reach out our hand to others with
flowers of compassion.

You are a miraculous blessing.

WE ARE PEACE

Lasting peace is inner peace, and

the more we master it, the more we assist in creating a

more peaceful collective.

Real strength and real knowledge come from within.

Learn to commune with yourself often.

Everything

is within us.

We only need to remember.

See yourself

Recognize yourself

See others

Recognize the other

Love yourself.

Learn to love in the face of all obstacles.

Learn to become your own master.

You are the master

and you are the keyholder -

Open.

Here for Love

As is water, so is life.

The waves may test our strength as

the ocean currents too may test our balance.

The little splashes of wet sand may test our inner humor

Let it test you

Stay the course

Being grounded is purely a state of mind

connection helps.

Stay connected to all that nurtures your Soul, and

release into the mystical stormy waters all that has served

its place.

We are here to love and be loved, and absolutely nothing

less.

Go ahead and walk into the waters
knowing that the only certainty in life
lies in miracles.

We are a miracle.

OPENING TO ANSWERS

Within, all mysteries are awaiting

to come forth and be revealed.

In all experiences, our unique Soul is expressing itself

to discover the beauty

revealed.

In life everything is a continuous choice.

We are the reason for it all.

We are the gift, the creation for through which all is gifted.

We are limitless, and we are everything we could ever

hope for in each moment.

I love you as I love me

for in thee is we.

BREAK OPEN

Everything that breaks us, is everything that makes us.

Life molds us into sheer perfection.

Be not fearful of the heavy storms in life.

They are merely here to shape our dreams

and allow, our Soul

To unfold.

Inner Gifts Giving

There is nothing

you do not already know.

When willing to look for truth and accept it as a guiding

light.

The path is always given, and our compass

is within.

Tune in, and follow your own truth, always.

This life is a gift.

I LONG FOR OUR LIGHT

There are no problems.

There are only empowered solutions.

Sometimes change arrives to realign us -

it always comes and goes while dancing with our Soul.

Just as our hearts can break to learn how to beat,

change ushers in the dances we need.

Everything is a newborn gift,

a new chance.

Everything leads the way -

Through darkness

opening to light.

Compassion, forgiveness and inner sight

usher us into the ever-twinkling starlight.

Sparkle for me, for it is such a delight.

Goddess Knows

What it is, in the depths of our Souls

as a river shall flow

Our directions too unfold.

Goddess knows

the birth as the death

Opens our Souls

to divinity

within our sacred

Whole

Souls know.

Love knows.

Goddess knows.

Into the Earth

108 feet deep

All goes

which does not

Bless Us.

Bless your

Mother

Daughter

Lover

Wife

For Goddess

so delights

when your birth

breeds insight.

108 feet deep

Goddess knows

within that

which we weep

Our Soul reaps.

Love yourself

Love others

Be

Honest

Kind

Loving -
Stay in the light
for it is so bright.

Goddess knows
and blesses

our Soul.

Reflections of our Sun

Like the sun, we rise in all our glory and splendor.

As the sun, we seek the shade of the clouds during stormy

moments in our lives.

If the sun remained constant and bright, missing

would be some

beautiful changes and transformations that take shape

during moments of retreat.

Like the sun, we pull back as we set intentions anew to

reawaken with the morning dew.

Allow yourself the same space as you allow our sun.

Master your life as the setting sun.

No one can steal your light as no one too can truly

withhold life -

make this life count.

Always give yourself the very love and respect you

deserve.

You are a miracle, just as grand as the rising and setting

sun.

You are a supernova.

Take flight, for you are so bright!

Open to Receive

Dance with

the fading grasses.

Nourish your Soul,

as the leaves surrender to all the beauty

of the fall.

Nature accepts and loves us,

just as we are

in each passing moment

of this breath.

Open your heart,

fall into her loving embrace.

Walk through the passageway of your increasingly

expansive heart.

As nature, the heart too embraces every part of you,

open

this me and you -

Paint your Soul.

Beauty all Around

Waiting at our doorstep,

we merely need to open the door.

Walk out to

open to the new within me and you.

Beauty lets light in while opening us up to

Love, love, love -

loving

within

and so without.

The sun warms our hearts while beautifying our Soul.

Open skies are open arms when we surrender to its

embrace.

Open mind, Soul embrace

Leaves fall and nourish us all

as soil becomes rich with the rootedness of All.

Every cycle awaits us with a kiss.

Luscious and luxurious is each moment,

"Receive me", says the spirit of the breath.

What is Love?

How do you love?

Who are you?

Let the light shine into your Soul

and teach you the ancient teachings

of the Master within.

Awaken to your purpose

Why are you here?

Life is ready to live through you.

When will you give in?

Give in, to Her love and teachings

Be the sun

Be the moon

Be the stars.

Be it all,

dearest child who we love

you know you have come far -

Arrival is here.

OPEN TO THE JOURNEY

Life, whimsical and magical

placing one foot after another

within our mind

we create and birth, the path we take.

Upon physical arrival, the presentation of this

manifestation

grander than our internal vision, we need only

open and expand to see.

Animals appear as guides

flowers uplift us with their emotionally healing

high vibrational scent.

The sky reveals guidance through patterned messages, and

the Earth blesses our feet.

All needs and wants are met

upon asking we receive.

Blessed are we to

take the step.

Walk with purpose upon the path.

HONOR SOUL FLOWER

Fully decide now

Honor yourself by honoring your path

Soul, together with Universal support and collaboration,

will fully direct and guide the path.

Fully supported, the road will be paved

Gold, when you decide to follow your deepest longings in

alignment with the good for all.

Follow what brings you joy, that is where the magic is, and

there is where you come alive.

What have you longed to do and be?

Decide that now is the time to gift the world with your

magnificence.

There is no turning back.

You are a forward moving

beam of light

a Star.

THE MEDICINE

No matter where we are on our unique journey, we have a

purpose.

When discovered, we know what our true medicine is

for which we are to offer up

to ourselves and the world.

Why follow someone else's teaching when you are here to

follow

the teachings of your heart and Soul?

Why study the medicine of another, when your own

sacred medicine

is a healer.

When we live with true compassion and love for ourselves

and others,

it opens us to enlightenment.

Allow the medicine in your Soul to rise
while waking up to know, you are wise.

Accept your calling. Flutter your wings
and fly, walk and move into eternity.

And, just as importantly, love yourself.

Teach us your ways medicine man and woman.

Let us taste your healing nectar.

The Tree of Life, Within

Be the tree

The tree of life

Is within you

Direct your awareness

Deep within the Mother -

Mother Earth, Pacha Mama

Connect your mind, heart, body and emotions

Accept your full empowerment

Activate your ability to expand;

While only accepting and being truth

Consciousness.

Amplify yourself

Feel our connectedness

Beneath and within the Mother -

Mother Earth, Pacha Mama;

For it is there that our roots unite.

All the portals

To all there is;

And all there ever was,

Is within you.

Love, wisdom and power

Is you and is within you.

Integrate it all

Accept nothing less

And know,

There is always more.

Feel the gratitude

Be your 'I Am' Presence

Direct and integrate

This into all aspects of your Beingness

Allow the tree within you to grow

45

Feel more harmony and peace

Fear not to release your leaves

Fear not to drop the branches

And all for which weighs you down

For you are the tree

You will grow more

And new leaves will appear

And shape your Soul

As new branches too

Shall grow

Allow the sun

To shine

Through you and within you

Be the tree

The tree of life

Is within you.

SHE

Another night, under the moonlight

She speaks to me

The language appears to me

As a dream

In a dream

Asked to carry forth with a vision

A great path is presented

The waters to get there are not easy

I navigate

I ask

I doubt

Oh, but I must doubt the doubt

Just as our great Maharishi had said

She says, "you are in the water, flow

swim through it

and soon

yes, very soon

you shall be freedom horse

and you will meet the great wise tree."

I continue

feeling strong, growing in courage

I navigate the waters

I turn around

to see

Oh, my journey

Soul and friend

is there -

A little behind;

Yet, navigating

as I am.

Can I do it?

Images of things and people

Once known

situations

Once scorned

I float past

deeper

into the vast

I reach the edge

of a great cliff -

Great glowing waters appear

I jump

No thoughts are there

I fall

into the depths

of the waters

What if I don't resurface?

Will I have air to breathe?

I appear

above it all

To my right is the grandest of trees

so strong yet so soft and tender

I rest

Looking back

to everything else -

To the Soul waiting above

at the water's edge

I cry out, "jump"

Silence

The journey must continue

The path is clear

The doubts have faded

The Soul is healed

My guides and ancestors ride with me

As I am now freedom horse

The call is answered

The tribe awaits

We dance upon the water.

Awakening to Dawn

Dawn is near

Here I meet you
Here I greet you

In this sacred
Infinite space

Oh, how I feel your embrace.

It is to taste the greatness

of your mistakes -

Your sweet songs of joy

Of a love

To which I awe;

For, with such a love

Nothing is a loss

Lessons learned
Journeys that burn
With the flame
Which is the only truth

The unspoken word.

I see you
I feel you
Inside my Soul
We meet

You walk with me
Guide me
To the gate
of our wisdom
Our truth
Where love has always overcome

We burn with the light of infinite

Skies

Nights

Songs

Poems

Love

Together,

We open

The wisdom

Gate

Heart

Soul

Spirit

Connect me

Unite me

To the infinite space

Love

Of infinite Oneness

Here

I love you

We meet

Embrace
Taste

Infinite Oneness
Open the door
The sacred gate

Have faith

For it is never too late to wake up
Dawn is near.

ROSE ESSENCE

Embrace your love.

Look into a rose and see your Soul

Breathe with a rose and feel eternal love

Sing with the rose, and you take flight

Spread your ecstatic wings and sing with us.

IN THE MORNING SUN

I see myself

My true Self

I have served you

I have loved you

My beloved Soul

Who I was yesterday

Who I am today

Who I become

With the rising

Sun

I rise with you

Beloved

Soul

Space

Within

Tell me

Whisper in my ear

Your truth

Tell me

When will the white buffalo come?

The prayers

Sweetest of dreams

Of those before us

Of all here now

Of those yet to come

I look

To the sacred

Four directions

Father Sky

Mother Earth

Together

We breathe

Oh, White Buffalo

Calf Woman

Return

We are ready

Past

Present

Future

To usher in

New times

New energies

Give us signs

Show us the way

Balance

Miracles

We are ready

Higher Self

Greater forces

Of the Universe

Breathe us forward

We wait no longer

We are the ones

We call upon you

White buffalo

Higher Self

Beloved Soul

Secure us in your

Strength

Faith

Great

Will power

We breathe

We are ready

For it is you

It is me

We are white buffalo

Calf Woman

Before you

Wait no longer for the other

Awaken

Feel your great strength

In the morning sun

We see ourselves

Our true Self

Beloved

Now we dance.

GIVING & RECEIVING

I am dreaming

A beautiful dream

With you

In gratitude

I am dreaming

Where dreams

Are miraculous

Miracles

Come true.

Love ignites

Soul light

Your candle

Burns

Even in the night

Angels of grace

Beings of the space

Flowers atop

The mountain top

The spark

Of the infinite heart

Bestow your

Gifts

Bestow

Your blessings

Give

Receive

Swim with the dolphins

Dream their dream

Embrace the infinite

Sky

Within and without.

My Beloved

Grateful

For you

For me

For parallel

Universes

I

We

Thee

I am grateful

For infinite skies

Blessings in disguise

Burning infinite grace

For which I need not even chase

Blessings

Blessed

Mother

Earth

Father

Sky

Two legged

Four legged

Winged ones

Bless you

Bless me

Fly with me

Fly within me

For now I see

It is you

Within me.

LOVE

The blissful kiss,

Of the soft

Breeze

Love

We are love

We belong to love

Love, belongs to us

Love

Infinite kiss

Of the sky

I give into you

I receive you,

giving thanks for you

Breathe

We are free

Here

And now

Love

It will never let you go

It will always bless your Soul

Come

Be

Receive

My kiss

For I am

Forever

Grateful

For your infinite

Embrace

For which

I taste

I give thanks.

ONE WITH THE SETTING SUN

The wind, the earth, the dust

The sky, the sun, the heavens

Mold us into shape

Give us perception -

Here and now

Instilling passion and poetry

Myth and astrology

Into our Souls

With a vision

For us to grow,

Molding wisdom

Into the depths of our Soul

When will the time come

For us to share

All we know

Infinite one

Come to me

Speak to me

We are One.

Subtle Infinite Space

Where our words reach the sky

Our heart opens

Everything expands

In this subtle awareness

Voices need not be heard

They are felt,

Without a sound

Within you is a key

The master key

To the master suite

All you need to do

Is open.

Find the opening

The spark that is you,

Is always there

Time and space

Infinity

You

Me

We

One

When this opening is revealed

Found

Is your sacred heart

Spiritual heart

Earth

Heaven

Sky

Peace

Love

It is all there

The wind

Becomes your lips

The sun

Becomes your eyes

The earth

Becomes your feet

The echoes of your Soul

Become your ears

Taste

See

Feel

Walk

We meet.

WALK

Keep moving

No need to ever look back

Walk

Feel the Earth under your feet

Feel the feelings

That once felt like defeat

Leaving meaning

In the imprints

Of your souls

Walk

With the Universe

On your back

Walk

Journey

Trust

Receive

Walk

Into infinity

With me

Walk

There is nowhere to be

Walk

You are with me

Walk

Feel my embrace

Feel the echoes

Of eternities grace

Walk

Walk with me

There is no place to be

But here

Soul

I see you

I feel you

I am you

Embrace

We meet

I see you

I feel you

In me

Walk

We are not alone

Infinity in the sky

Eternity on our shoulders

Faith on the path

Trust on our back

Walk with me

For there is no turning back

Walk

Stay the path.

The Circle of Love

Life is a circle

Wherein, there is love.

All are included

Embraced through Soul eyes

Rainbows of light

Fill our hearts

When we sparkle with delight

Upon the opening in sight:

A portal,

A Window

Into all hearts

Of a unified heart

All are connected, just as

Flowers bloom

Trees grow

Fragrance abound

I lay down

Still it beats

The sound of heaven

All within a heartbeat.

Dance with my Soul

Embrace the rays

All within our days

Of understanding and love.

CHANGE

Could it be

Desire

Passion;

Could it be

The call

Destiny

Could you, Soul,

Be yearning,

For

Momentum

Spark

Courage

The moment

Divine light

Divine change

With

Seasons

Planets

Stars

The Infinite

True heaven on Earth

Awaits

Listen

Go within

The heart

Knows

The way

Will we listen?

Take heed

Look around

Everywhere

Is Love

Take heed

Open

to change and reveal your heart to the world.

What are you waiting for?

For, you shall be received.

THE SECRET CALL

Secretly, they call us in the night,

beings of golden white light.

Purple rays upon our crowns, all while we rest

our head in bed.

Dragons of orange vibration, reawakening our memory of

our creation.

We awaken with a feeling of bliss, all within the night time

kiss.

The secrets have been revealed, opened and no longer lay

dormant inside.

We call upon you to carry the light on beyond the night.

Awaken the spirit that is you

for you will be received in the purple glow all around you.

Burn on heart, and reawaken within us your presence.

Call upon us secretly in the night.

Heart of Hearts, Speak

Feel your truth, as an echo in the wind.

What you feel, holds the secrets
waiting to be revealed.

It is a key, an opening, a possibility

Magic awaits, when we embrace our truth.

Oh dearest heart, meet me, see me, speak with me.
Keep your door open, walk me through the gate. What else
is there to truly await?

Turn the key. Unleash your truth and wisdom.

Spill out upon me dearest moon, awaken within me, all

while I bloom.

As the sun shines upon you moon, you too shine upon my

Soul.

Heart, we are here. Now we walk.

EMBRACE

Change

Grow

Expand

Love -

Open your heart

The trees love us, just as we are.

The earth carries us, no matter how far.

Our hearts stay with us and love us, and never truly let us

down.

The only thing that matters, is the love and acceptance we

have for ourselves.

How much do we laugh, love,

sing with nature, and embrace the gifts

of those we love,

and give out blessings of our love?

Dress up, dress down, take it off, be the clown

You are beautiful, just as you are.

The wind, the sky, the sun

They love us and support us

No matter how we are.

Chase your dreams, follow the stars, go to mars

Whose life? Your life.

You are living the dream. Your dream.

Go on. It will take you far.

Keep going.

TRANSCEND

Escape the dream you have created

To dream anew

Dreams

And wishes, come true

When there is nothing to do

Dream

Open your heart

And open your eyes

To the new way of being

Dream

If only for a little while

Feel

All you are meant to be

See

The dreamed dream

Oh, such pleasure

Oh, such delight

For nothing is out of sight

Dream

Open your eyes

For it shall appear,

There is nothing to fear

Dream

Be not dreamed. Be the dreamer.

Awaken.

WAKE UP

For the dawn is here,

The moment is near

Call upon your

Guides

Spirit

Higher Self

The sun within each

And every

One

Of us

Will rise and shine

Release,

Free yourself

Lay down

Your arms

Surrender

To the embrace

Of infinity

All within

This taste

Of love and freedom

Release

Now

Walk with me

Talk with me

Be with me

Breathe with me

Spirit

Guide me.

RISE UP

From anything

even that

which you did not know

was weighing you down

Rise up

walk with me

talk with me

You shine so bright

in my Soul

Bright

even in the night

Feel the release

set your Soul free

Breathe

in and out

with me.

Together

we fly

soaring high

Looking back

all the weight

left behind;

Our ancestors

guide us

as we return to the light -

Embrace.

Soak your Soul

It is all you will ever need to know.

Stay there -

Embrace

each and every moment

as a kiss from great spirit.

This time

Tender to the heart,

embraced by the Soul

it is all we really need to know.

Open

to loves embrace

Know

with all your heart

and all your Soul

You are loved.

Open your heart, and watch life ignite

Feast in joy

Be in love

Release it all to the moment

and be at peace.

SACRED SPACE

The thorns

all within

I pulled you out

Every sliver of infinite grace

I need not even give haste

I feel you

I return to you

In this sacred space

even your thorns give me mercy

and never leave me thirsty.

The chill in the air

The warmth of the sun

The taste of this day

Oh, how shall I be unspun.

She weaves me anew

Sacred and true

Naked to her strength

I hear anew

I need not even seek you

for, you are here with me.

Infinite space

Sacred hums

Where all returns to One

The truths revealed

The lessons unraveled

Seeker of time

I need not even travel

All is here

with this One

Sacred Love -

Sacred Embrace.

Taste this Tree

Even if her elixir is your distaste

Misunderstood

Yes, at times

Though she knows her sap is divine.

Climb the bark

Go deep with her

Open up to her divine elixir

In this moment

of infinite embrace

You may never know

unless you

Taste

Infinity

Ecstasy

Sanctity

Open to her love

Mother Nature heals

Oh what a thrill

Heal with us

Be with us

Listen

Her mystery is calling

You

Me

We

Us

Listen.

AGLOW

We are made of light photons, quantum electromagnetic

energy all within

and around us.

Live your life as such.

To play it small, is truly against our nature and non-

beneficial to our physical, emotional and spiritual well-

being.

Why do anything against our very nature when we can

take the step and leap into our greatness?

It is effortless to live a life for and in support of life.

Show us your light.

Represent your true Self.

Never back down.

Let us hear you roar while you show us your light.

Demonstrate your truth and set the way aglow for All.
Society will follow in your footsteps, and all shall ignite in
ecstatic high-vibrational energy and joy.

Yes, we shall reclaim our birthright.

It is happening.

It is here.

Now is the moment.

Glow.

THE THRESHOLD

Walking

Through the end

The beginning is near

Forever seeing clear

With each step and each breath

The Soul expands and yearns

To be a part of creation

To serve you

Each turn

Every flicker of light

It offers such delight.

The threshold

The point of no return

Ever so near

There is nothing to fear.

Walk with me

Sweet spirit

Standing amongst the flower

Ever reflecting the light

Embracing the sweet fragrance

The sacred vibrations

Turn your Soul

Awaken the spirit

An opening

Has been there all along

Walk

Trust

Embrace

The mystery

Know

The beginning is the end. The end is the beginning.

Awaken

The only truth

Is infinity

The flower

The one

Sacred breath

And beauty

All are one

We awaken

We are the One

We see

Our true divinity

Oh, sacred one

We are One.

Take the sacred step

Breathe the infinite scent

Return to who you are

And awaken in this state.

WE ARE NEVER ALONE

Stepping up, the game, as if there are no winners nor

losers.

Simply, players within a field, unified

In conscious love.

Aware of the stakes

Connected to those

Playing for a better way

For all to see clear.

Flourishing into a river from the heart

To the Soul -

A nation

Undivided,

Unified in a field

Of conscious play, with

Never-ending

Love, for our great nation.

A magnificent player

Playing fair, with all

Stepping up, in our glorious world

Within a planet

Of conscious

Global natives.

Our inter-connected world,

Supported by sovereign Beings - our vote is our word.

About the Author

Ulonda Faye is a political scientist, healer and lover of life. In 2012, she had a Near Death Experience (NDE), which completely altered the course of her life. From this new perspective and infinite resource, our interconnectedness became clear and known to her. She has integrated her experience dying with her professional experience in politics, the healing arts and spiritual science to bring forth writing that unifies us.

For more information, please visit:

www.UlondaFaye.com

Made in the USA
Coppell, TX
09 May 2021

55294453R00066